Contents

1. A collection of carved ivory hatpins.

Introduction

A JEWEL is created primarily as a form of self-adornment with the jeweller endeavouring both to enhance the beauty of the wearer and to show off his skill and flair as a craftsman. One of the greatest qualities of a jewel is its ability to reflect the personality and tastes of the owner. It is a highly personal and individual form of decoration which can, in some cases, combine its aesthetic qualities with a rather more practical and useful purpose, namely that of securing some form of garment. Both hatpins and tiepins are designed for this purpose and the 19th and early 20th century saw the creation of a vast repertoire of these jewels (figs. 1–4). This was an exciting period, witnessing rapid changes both socially and technically and the jeweller was eager as well as able to accommodate every passing whim in fashion and taste which accompanied these pioneering days.

2. (*left*) A rose diamond horse and jockey tiepin, *c.*1900.

3. (*centre*) An enamelled trout tiepin, *c.*1900.

4. (*right*) A rose diamond swan tiepin, *c.*1900.

1. Hatpins

HATPINS were in use throughout the 19th century but until virtually the end of the century hat ties took precedence over the pin as a means of holding the hat in place. It was not until the early years of the 20th century that the hatpin really came into its own, both as a means of securing the hat and as a vital fashion accessory. Its years of glory spanned a relatively short period, rising in size and popularity from about 1905 and declining in both with the outbreak of war in 1914.

A hatpin merely consists of a decorative head attached to a pin. The form which the head took could vary from the sublime to the ridiculous as well as including classic

5. (*left*) A glass hatpin, *c*.1920.

6. (*right*) A glass hatpin, overlaid with gold decoration, *c*.1920.

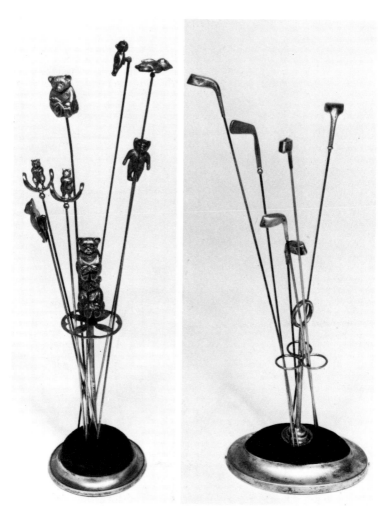

7. (*left*) A collection of silver teddy bear hatpins 1905–10, several showing flip tops, on a silver hatpin holder.

8. (*right*) A collection of silver 'golfing' hatpins, the heads in the form of golf clubs.

or simple designs and was crafted from all manner of materials. The slender pin was most commonly made from tempered steel but gold, silver, brass or base metals were also used. Depending on the material used for it, the head could be attached to the pin by a variety of methods. Materials such as pearls, coral or glass could be drilled through the base and the pin cemented in, or in the case of the latter, it could be sunk in while the glass was still molten, being secured as the material cooled and contracted (fig. 5). Often the head was attached by a special foot (fig. 6) or was riveted to a base, or the base and foot were made in one piece and joined to the top. The pin was then sunk into these attachments. They often sported flip-tops which enabled the right side of the pin to be on show whichever side of the hat it was worn (fig. 7).

9. A collection of hatpins, the heads including pastes, mother of pearl and amethysts, showing the variety of lengths from the late 19th century until 1914.

10. A pair of Satsuma hatpins.

Obviously the nature and fashionableness of the hatpin relied quite heavily upon the style and mode of the hat as well as upon the popular designs in other forms of jewellery of the same period. For the 19th and early 20th century woman it was both extremely rare and quite unseemly to be seen in public without a hat whatever her social standing. Indeed during the greater part of the 19th century it was even deemed improper to go around the home without some form of head covering. Lace caps or, as they were more frequently known, boudoir caps, often fulfilled the indoor role and the elderly still clung to this symbol of propriety until the beginning of the 20th century. The 19th century was the age of the hat and the bonnet, which continually vied with each other for popularity. The main difference between the two was that a bonnet was either brimless or had a small brim around the front and was usually the preserve of married women or those who had been presented to society.

The first half of the 19th century saw great changes in the size and shape of headwear for women which was held in place by ties and rather short-stemmed plain silver or gold hat-

11. (*below*) Three Satsuma hatpins.

12. (*above*) A porcelain hatpin, decorated with a transfer print of a pastoral scene.

pins. By the 1870s and 1880s small bonnets and hats were resting precariously on the peaks of elaborate coiffures built up with false hair and wire concealed by garlands of flowers and ribbons. Although this form of headwear was usually tied beneath the chin it could also be secured by a hatpin, still very simple, the head of gold, silver, jet or pearl, and the stem now required to be slightly longer. The other bonnets of that period were embellished by an amber headed pin. The late 1880s saw tall hats extravagantly adorned with ribbons, aigrettes and even stuffed birds once again kept in place with ties, usually ribbon, or speared with hatpins which now included heads of cut steel or bronze beads. But by the 1890s the ties had had their day and the hatpin now reigned supreme and alone. Both small and large hats, still outrageously decorated,

13. (*left*) A tortoiseshell piqué hatpin.

14. (*centre*) A tortoiseshell hatpin.

15. (*right*) A tortoiseshell piqué hatpin.

10

16. A tortoiseshell piqué hatpin.   17. A tortoiseshell piqué hatpin.

were pinned firmly to the head by even longer hatpins which went through the crown of the hat and out again at the other side. But still they had not reached the amazing lengths of the immediate pre-war years.

However, hatpins were becoming adventurous and a host of more inspired designs took the place of the rather conservative earlier examples. Hats were now created for the many activities which previously had been the domains of men. The more liberated woman emerging towards the beginning of the 20th century could now engage freely in such sports as golf (fig. 8), tennis and cycling and even turn her hand to the steering wheel of a car, and hats were designed to suit each occasion. The hats made for motoring usually incorporated a heavy veil which completely covered the face, protecting the complexion against the dust and pollution disturbed from the very primitive roads.

By the end of the 1890s hats with extremely wide brims were already in vogue and the following years experienced such a rapid increase in their size that by about 1911 it

18. (*left*) A pair of mosaic hatpins.

19. (*right*) A moulded black glass 'bonnet' hatpin.

20. A gilt metal and mosaic hatpin with corded wire decoration.

appeared they could expand no further. The hat, as always highly decorated, had become the main feature of the female dress; indeed it was so vast and so nearly preposterous that it became the focal point of either the onlooker's admiration or ridicule.

Obviously during this era of enormous hats hatpins were a necessity and they were made in vast quantities in a whole range of designs. The size of the hatpin (fig. 9) altered with the size of the hat and from 1911 until the War it reached the absurd lengths of between 14 and 16 inches. Indeed it became almost lethal. Numerous cases were reported throughout Britain and the Continent of accidental injuries received from hatpins: eyes were poked out and people stabbed. The hatpin also had its uses as a weapon in both fiction and in real life. In England questions were asked in Parliament and council meetings about the dangers which lay in the female hat. Certain city councils adopted by-laws to prevent women wearing hatpins with unprotected points in any public place and equivalent laws were adopted throughout Europe. Correspondence on the subject appeared in *The Times* during the Spring of 1914 and it was obviously a great worry to the British public at large as the writer of one rather verbose letter pointed out, signing himself 'One for All'. Some women did abide by the advice to wear pin protectors and either fitted on a special dart or bead-shaped end, or a motif which matched the design of the hat. The less affluent used small corks. The making of pin protectors did not seem to catch on very well with British manufacturers and they were mainly imported from the Continent.

During the First World War the size of the hat decreased and the immediate post-war years saw the vogue for close-fitting simple cloche hats. These did not require securing with hatpins but the habit of wearing them did not die so easily: hatpins were worn mainly as

21. A moulded black glass 'strawberry' hatpin.

22. A collection of butterfly hatpins made from various materials.

23. (*left*) A gold and *champlevé* enamel hatpin of a nude nymph by René Lalique.

24. (*right*) A gold and *plique-à-jour* enamel hatpin of a lilac coloured clover, by René Lalique.

25. A gold plated hatpin designed as the head of a female warrior, French.

decorative embellishments. The pins became much shortened and protectors were used more as a prevention against loss than against accidents. However, by the end of the 1920s the hat itself was being discarded and although even today it is still an attractive accessory to the female attire it has never again become the necessary feature of every-day life that it once was. Thus the hatpin was no longer required.

A great variety of hatpins was made during the late 19th century and early years of the 20th century just before the real hatpin vogue. Porcelain in particular enjoyed great popularity. The taste for the Orient had been evoked recently and Japanese satsuma hat-pins were extremely popular (fig. 10). Most of this porcelain is glazed in soft hues of brown, cream and yellow and decorated with pastel-coloured oriental motifs such as dragons, ornamental flowers or fabulous birds (fig. 11), often outlined in gold. Satsuma hatpin heads were usually sent over from Japan and mounted here in England. This was also the case with much European porcelain. French porcelain especially, was highly fashionable for hatpin heads (fig. 12). A common example is a spherical head decorated with a transfer print, or hand painted with a charming little pastoral scene or flowers. The quality and attractiveness of these hatpins varies enormously. Unfortunately, although vast quantities were made, very few are marked and with so many similar European styles it is impossible to pinpoint where exactly they were produced. Examples were also made in English factories.

Another highly successful material used for hatpins of this period was tortoiseshell. It does not, in fact, come from the tortoise but from the epidermic plates of the hawksbill turtle. These are heated to a certain temperature and

26. A gold, jade, enamel and diamond hatpin, attributed to Peter Carl Fabergé.

27. A collection of silver hatpins of scroll designs, some by the firm of Charles Horner.

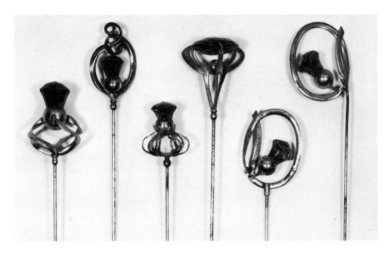

28. A collection of silver hatpins of thistle designs, set with pastes and amethysts.

then immersed in boiling water until they become sufficiently malleable to be pressed into the required shape. Colours are usually shades of red, brown and yellow, the latter often mottled. Plain tortoiseshell was often moulded into interesting shapes (fig. 14) or simple beads to form hatpins, but sometimes it was decorated with piqué work (figs. 13 and 15). This technique had been introduced into England by the Huguenots in the 17th century and it was revived by 18th and 19th century jewellers. While the process of moulding the tortoiseshell is taking place and the material is still warm a design is drawn in dots on the surface. These dots are then drilled and filled with minute amounts of gold or silver. As the shell cools and contracts the metal is gripped in place. Originally the process was all done by hand but by the end of the 19th century machinery had been developed to produce very fine quality piqué work. The hatpins were

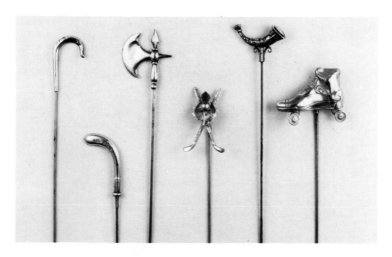

29. A group of silver hatpins including a shepherd's crook, a hockey stick, a pike, crossed hockey sticks, a horn and a skating boot.

in a variety of shapes, from spherical to flat rectangles and the decoration included geometric as well as delicate floral designs (figs. 16 and 17).

The revival of mosaic jewellery also came to the head of the hatpin towards the end of the century. The mosaic was usually Roman and came in a number of different shapes and designs, floral motifs perhaps being the most popular (fig. 18). These were often embellished with corded wire or granulation work and set in a base of gilt metal (fig. 20). On the whole, the mosaic, although still extremely colourful, was rather cruder than the majority of examples in earlier jewels. Jet, or imitation jet in the form of black glass, was especially useful as a material for hatpins during periods of mourning; the death of Queen Victoria in 1901 gave added impetus to this fashion (fig. 19). It was carved or moulded into designs varying from a simple button

30. A silver and amethyst hatpin designed as a sword by the firm of Charles Horner.

shape to more elaborate flowers and fruits (fig. 21). This period also saw the very popular butterfly and star motifs pavé-set with semi-precious stones such as moonstones, garnets or pastes, and mounted in both base and precious metals or decorated with enamel (fig. 22).

Two of the most important influences on jewellery at this time were the Arts and Crafts and the art nouveau movements. The Arts and Crafts movement was primarily initiated for the worker to rediscover the true meaning of craft and workmanship and to express once again his ideas through his hands. In 1888 the Arts and Crafts movement held its first exhibition, closely followed by the setting up of the Art Workers Guild and the Home Arts and Industries Association which endeavoured to introduce handiwork classes throughout the country. One of the greatest pioneers of this movement was the jeweller and silversmith C. R. Ashbee. He and others looked to nature for their inspiration and evoked its earthy qualities in their work whether it was an intricate design of scrolled foliage, a simple

31. A group of silver teddy bear hatpins.

32. A group of silver animal hatpins including a boxing monkey, a lion and a cockerel's head.

33. A silver vinaigrette hatpin.

flowerhead or an abstract design. This style was enthusiastically followed by both amateur and professional jewellers and some extremely well designed and skilfully executed pieces left the bench. Although hatpins from these jewellers are few and far between their influence on the designs of later examples is highly important. The hatpins were usually silver, sometimes set with semi-precious stones such as peridots or turquoise, decorated with enamel or set with an interestingly shaped baroque pearl. The heads were in designs such as elaborate scrolls, flowers or the typical peacock. The latter was one of C. R. Ashbee's most popular motifs and its distinctive blue and green coloration was represented in enamels which have become synonymous with Arts and Crafts jewels. Liberty and Company of London produced some charming hatpins of this type. It is also interesting to note that in this age of women's suffrage many of the most successful designers of the style were women.

Meanwhile across the Channel in France the art nouveau movement was in full swing. This form of design produced some exquisite

34. A group of hatpins by the firm of Charles Horner.

hatpins, again usually enamelled. One of the most gifted jewellers working in the style was René Jules Lalique (fig. 23). Although he worked in Paris he frequently returned to the countryside of his birth and, like members of the Arts and Crafts movement, gained enormous inspiration from nature, following and studying its changing patterns. With intense feeling he and many of the other art nouveau designers managed to captivate the colours and moods of nature in their work. Lalique's favourite warm and yet rather sombre autumnal tones worked remarkably well whether executed in enamels or carved in horn. More than almost any other jeweller he investigated the full possibilities of the materials available to him. *Plique à jour* enamel was one of his strengths (fig. 24). This form of enamel is not backed and therefore if held up to the light it has the serene and splendid appearance of a stained glass window. Lalique's hatpins took the form of many kinds of animals, flowers and insects which decorated the hat.

Other disciples of art nouveau included the House of Vever whose typical hatpin designs

35. A pair of silver suffragette hatpins.

36. A hatpin set, decorated with enamel.

included the nude female, and Lucien
Gaillard who produced exquisite examples
both in carved horn and enamel. Another
characteristic French hatpin was formed from
a medallion struck like a coin from gold, silver
or gold-plate (fig. 25). It often depicted the
head of a woman with an elaborate coiffure or
headdress and sometimes, in the same vein as
the gem-set cameo habillés, the woman wore
some form of jewellery set with rose diamonds.
Sadly, the new century saw the gradual demise
of both the Arts and Crafts and art nouveau
movements. They were styles which required
jewellers of imagination as well as skill and
unfortunately for a time this kind of innovative
craftsman was lost.

Meanwhile in America Louis Comfort
Tiffany was extremely successful in intro-
ducing the art nouveau style and his Broad-
way shop sold some delightful hatpins, among
the most popular designs being enamelled
butterflies and dragonflies. From Russia came
the wonderful hatpins of Peter Carl Fabergé
(fig. 26). His designs and enamelling techniques were superb and he often used his skill

in this capacity to decorate his hatpins, sometimes further embellishing them with minute carved hardstone animals.

Some of the most successful hatpins made between 1905 and 1914 were mass produced in both precious and base metals. They were thus available to women from every social class. The start of the new century saw the silver trade once again highly active in Britain and vast quantities of silver hatpins were produced. These were mainly assayed at Birmingham and Chester but also at other offices such as London and Sheffield. The heads came in an enormous variety of forms,

37. A group of enamelled hatpins.

38. A pair of *guilloché* enamel hatpins.

many of which were patented by the makers. The Arts and Crafts influence is seen in the popular scroll and knot motifs (fig. 27), sometimes entwined around a thistle set with various quartz or pastes (fig. 28). The current female preoccupation with sporting activities was catered for and hatpins appeared in the form of sporting equipment and related objects such as golf clubs, hockey sticks or skating boots (fig. 29). A silver dagger or sword-like pin was fashionable for securing the motoring habit (fig. 30). The hats of hunting, shooting and fishing ladies were furnished with fishing flies, pieces of stag horn or grouse claws all mounted in silver, perhaps as a souvenir of a successful day's sport.

On one occasion President Theodore Roosevelt, a keen hunter, was seen by members of the press spearing a bear cub and the incident was rapidly publicized, initially in the form of a cartoon in the *Washington Post* in November, 1902. In 1903 in New York Maurice Michtom started regular production of the soft toy which was immediately christened the 'Teddy' bear after the President. These soon appeared as rather adorable silver hatpins either sitting or stand-

39. (*below*) A collection of enamelled butterfly hatpins.

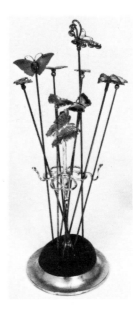

ing alone or in pairs on the top of some exotic creation (fig. 31). A whole zoological garden was built up for the hatpin with animals such as lions, boxing monkeys and hens creating rather an enchanting if somewhat bizarre effect (fig. 32). A more useful silver hatpin came in the form of a spherical vinaigrette or pin holder (fig. 33).

The company of Charles Horner was one of the most renowned and prolific manufacturers of hatpins (fig. 34). This was a Halifax firm and their products were usually assayed in Birmingham or Chester, the latter more· fre-

40. A group of enamelled hatpins, including a swallow and three abstract designs in the Arts and Crafts style.

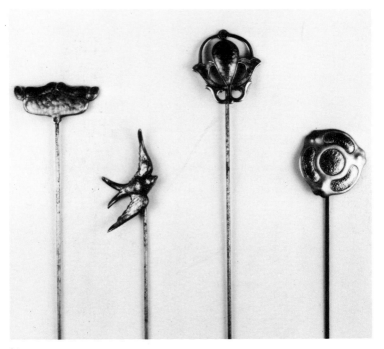

42. (*below*) A collection of cut and moulded glass hatpins.

quently for the simple reason that the assay office was open more often. Charles Horner himself had died in 1896 but the business was carried on by his son. Most of the firm's hatpins were produced during the first decade of the 20th century. Their range was vast and although a great many of their hatpins do not appear very much out of the ordinary, one does occasionally see an exceptional piece of silversmithing bearing the CH hallmark.

Silver hatpins depicting suffragettes were also produced. These were presumably made to be worn by the champions of the cause whose motto was *E Pluribus Unum* ('Many made One') (fig. 35). Sometimes the silver tops of hatpins were enamelled, and the disc-shaped examples were frequently sold in velvet or silk-lined boxes as sets with matching buttons and brooches (fig. 36). The enamel was often *guilloché* which is a fairly translucent enamel through which a design engraved on the backing can be seen, giving a shimmery effect (figs. 37 and 38). Enamelled butterflies or birds could look extremely attractive fluttering around the head (figs. 39 and 40).

Another typical motif, often enamelled, was the swastika which might not appear so attractive today because of its close association with Hitler and the Nazis. The swastika was in fact a pre-Christian cross, being a religious emblem in India and China at least ten centuries before Christianity; it was also

43. Two hardstone and crystal hatpins.

thought of as an emblem of good luck, the word Svasti meaning well-being in Sanskrit. Without any of its more sinister connotations the swastika symbol did make very stylish hatpins.

Beaded heads came in many different materials including coral, amber, cut-steel, filigree and glass. Filigree is a type of decoration in which silver or gold threads are twisted together to form delicate lace-like patterns. These are either mounted freely or soldered to metal grounds (fig. 41). Glass was a highly successful material for the hatpin as it could be used in a whole variety of colours and shapes, often embellished with gold overlays in designs of flowers and scrolls (fig. 42). Glass hatpins of this type were produced in profusion throughout Europe as were a whole selection of glass animals and fruit.

Although precious stones were mounted as hatpins and indeed a single pearl or diamond could look extremely elegant, the majority of gem-set pins were mounted with less expensive and more commonplace stones such as moonstones, peridots and quartz, the latter being the generic term for such gems as

44. A collection of carved ivory hatpins designed as birds and animals.

45. Two glass hatpins, one designed as a bunch of grapes, the other as a pear-shaped bead.

citrine, amethyst, crystal and cairngorms (fig. 43). Brightly coloured pastes were also very useful for making hatpins for the cheaper end of the market.

Souvenir hatpins were made from materials which varied according to the resort they came from. Memories of a happy day by the sea could be recaptured by a polished pebble or a sea-shell mounted as a hatpin. These were often rather crudely mounted by being literally stuck to a base metal pin by a local trader. Connemara marble from Ireland, the various forms of quartz from Scotland and serpentine from Cornwall were all cut and polished to provide hatpin heads for lady visitors. However, for those who wished to suggest a more exotic holiday the head of a humming bird could nestle on the hat rather imposingly.

During the height of the hatpin vogue ivory was carved into animals, birds or flowers and then painted (fig. 44). Ivory was often imitated in celluloid, the first form of plastic to be used commercially. Hatpins could also be home-made from converted buttons lovingly mounted by the fireside. During and shortly after the War it became a craze to have military buttons mounted as hatpins. These were worn either in memory of a departed loved one or for the sweetheart still fighting in the muddy trenches. These are usually on shorter pins as by this time the size of the hat was diminishing and so was the length of the hatpin. After the War hatpins became simpler. They were usually sold in pairs and often took the form of a single pearl or a

46. Hatpin holders of ceramic and metal.

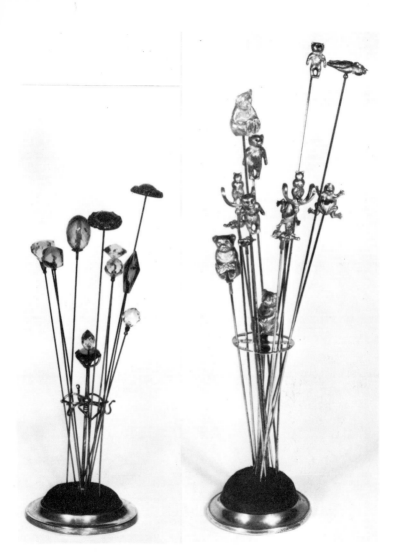

47. A silver-plated stand holding various paste hatpins; and a silver stand holding various teddy bear and frog hatpins.

jewelled bead. By the end of the 20s blown glass beads (fig. 45), glittering sequins mounted in cone shapes or the distinctive art deco plastic hatpins were all the rage but the fact remained that both the hat and the hatpin had had their day.

Unless it had its original box or a special card it was difficult to find an appropriate place to keep the hatpin where it would not prove hazardous, and the hatpin holder was designed to overcome this problem. These came in a whole variety of materials and designs. Ceramic holders shaped like canisters with holes in the top were produced and often sold with matching toilet sets which included basins, water jugs and various dishes and pots (fig. 46). Silver holders with weighted and padded bases and a series of loops for the pins to pass through appeared on the market; the central stem was often in one of the typical hatpin designs of the day such as a golf club or a teddy bear (fig. 47).

2. Tiepins

A TIEPIN is one of the few forms of jewellery which gives a man the opportunity to show off his flair in dress and indicate his personality to the world at large. The tiepin, together with the tie, can also provide a touch of light relief to otherwise dull and conventional male attire. Gone are the times when men could strut like peacocks in costumes which rivalled if not surpassed the extravagance of female dress. However, the tie of today does not always provide such a

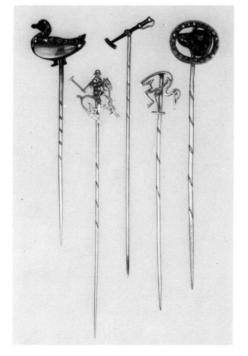

48. A collection of late 19th and early 20th century gold tiepins, several gem-set.

perfect setting for the tiepin as did the neck-wear of previous centuries. The necktie itself was basically designed as an eye-catching feature as it is the collar which keeps the neck warm and the outer garments clean. The neck attire of the 19th and early 20th centuries came in many guises but basically it took the form of the stock, the cravat or the tie (fig. 48).

The neckcloth came into being in the 17th century just before the advent of the three-piece suit. Before that a lace-edged collar attached to the shirt sufficed. The first neck-cloth was a lace-edged cravat. It was usually a square of lightly starched fine white material which was folded diagonally into a band and wound around the collar. The stock emerged in the late 17th century but did not achieve any popularity until the beginning of the 18th. It was a broad band of delicate material, sometimes stiffened with cardboard, tied around the neck. By the 1760s, the stock was

49. A collection of 18th and early 19th century memorial tiepins.

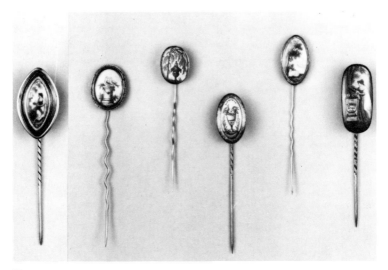

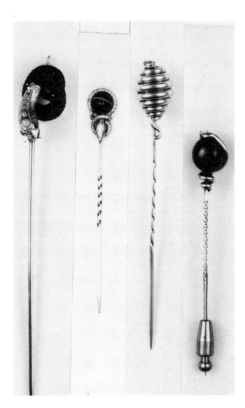

in vogue and the cravat had been relegated to more casual activities such as country walks or sports.

However, the beginning of the 19th century saw the return of the cravat to favour. The art of tying these cravats became something of a mania, stimulated by the influence of that king of young bucks and dandies, Beau Brummel. In 1828 H. le Blanc published a book giving detailed instructions and diagrams showing how to tie the cravat correctly. Each method had a different name and many required both skill and patience to accomplish. Indeed the cravat had probably become the most important item of male attire and the way in which it was tied indicated the refinement and even the breeding of the wearer: if the finished result was only perfected after one or even two hours it showed that the wearer was a true gentleman with time on his hands. Throughout the 19th century the cravat held its place in the male wardrobe but it frequently altered in shape and size. Its popularity only waned briefly between 1870 and 1880 when the outer

52. (*left*) A gold and sardonyx cameo of a lady's head.

53. (*right*) Two shell cameo tiepins.

garments were worn buttoned up to the neck.

In the 1860s the prototype of the modern tie, called a 'four in hand', emerged and this was well received by the male population because of its capacity to stay tidy and in place. The turn of the century still saw the cravat in its many different forms in pride of place, but the Edwardians popularized a whole host of different ties such as the Ascot, regimental, old school and club varieties as well as the bow tie, and these are still part of the male wardrobe of today. The Edwardian

54. (*above*) A carved coral cameo of a lady; and a carved coral cameo of the head of Christ.

55. (*left*) A carved coral cherub; a carved coral head of a god; and a carved coral dog.

man was extremely fashion-conscious, but sadly the War seemed to put an end to his rather flamboyant image. The post-war years saw his clothes becoming more and more drab until by around 1930 they really were very dreary.

All these fashions in neckwear were further enlivened and in most cases secured by the tiepin. Throughout the 19th and early 20th century the various forms and designs of tiepins closely followed the fashions in women's jewellery. When fashionable ladies were wearing diamond and enamel flower brooches the equally fashion-conscious gentlemen were wearing similar jewels in their cravats. The jeweller could thus produce his feminine creations in miniature for his male clientele.

Just like the hatpin, the tiepin comprises a

56. (*left*) Two coral tiepins, one entwined in a gold knot.

57. (*right*) Two Roman mosaic tiepins.

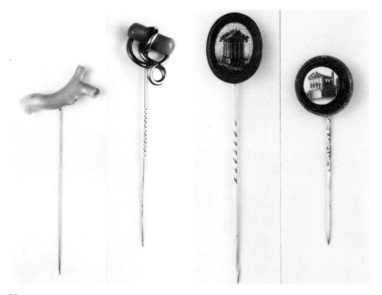

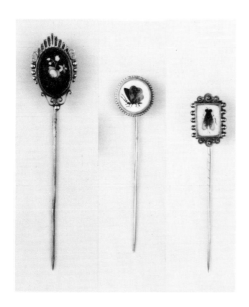

decorative head on the top of a pin, this being made from either precious or base metals. Again a protector was sometimes used either in the form of a butterfly which screwed on to the pin or a bobbin-shaped end piece. During the 18th century the pin was fairly short and in a zig-zag shape which must have played havoc with the fine material through which it was pushed and pulled. Fortunately by the 19th century the jeweller had fashioned a far simpler pin which, although still able to secure the neckwear, was kinder to the cloth. There was now just a short twist towards the top of the pin and even this feature was sometimes omitted.

During the 18th century tiepins were mainly either clusters of pastes or single stones. The pastes were usually pavé-set. The stones are dropped into holes drilled into the setting and then secured by minute rims of beads or metal. Single stone examples were

59. A collection of carved ivory tiepins.

60. (*below*) A gold and quartz flowerhead tiepin.

usually cut into a cushion shape or, in the case of many of the diamond pieces, rose cut and mounted in a closed setting. Here the stone was secured in the setting by a thin band of metal which was soldered to the mount. This was often of great advantage to the jeweller as the stone could be backed with a coloured foil or the back facets could be painted to enhance or give colour to a colourless stone. However, by the early 1800s it was found that, with diamonds especially, if the setting was left open a far greater amount of light could pass into and through the stone enabling it to show off its maximum brilliancy. The vogue for both of these tiepins lasted well into the 19th century; indeed the single stone continued to be fashionable throughout the century.

Another late 18th century craze which continued in the 19th century was for memorial

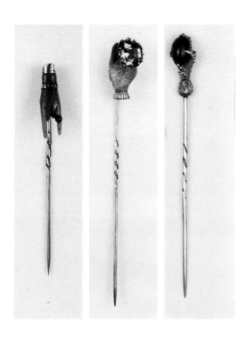

61. (*left*) A carved coral tiepin designed as a hand.

62. (*centre*) A gold and gem-set tiepin designed as a hand.

63. (*right*) A gold and carbuncle tiepin designed as an eagle's claw.

and mourning jewels. These jewels of senti-ment were keepsakes to be worn in memory of both the living and the dead. Queen Victoria's own long period of mourning for Prince Albert helped to stimulate the fashion for these jewels (fig. 49). The early 19th century memorial tie-pins were very much in the neo-classical mould, often taking the form of a gold and seed pearl urn, pearls being the symbol of tears; or a sepia miniature painted on ivory in a lozenge-, marquise- or oval-shaped mount. The miniature was totally enclosed by crystal or glass to withstand the effects of damp and dirt. It often depicted a somewhat melo-dramatic scene showing the bereft sighing over the tomb of the loved one with winged cherubs adding to the vision of desolation and despair. The initials of the departed were woven in gold thread, or a lock of his or her hair was incorporated into the picture with wistful words encircling the whole. These miniatures were usually mounted in gold, the border consisting of either a very plain Roman setting or of engraved motifs such as laurel leaves. Some were also decorated with enamel or set with pastes, pearls or rose diamonds which seem to add a touch of life to the rather gloomy effect. The reverse of the jewel often provides a most interesting feature: besides the typical engraved foliate decoration there is often a detailed inscription giving the name, and dates of birth and death of the deceased which can prove fascinating for those with an interest in genealogy.

However, throughout the 19th century styles in memorial jewellery altered. From the 1820s the pin simply had a cluster of garnets,

64. A gold and carved onyx head of a blackamoor, capped by a coral turban; a gold, enamel and chalcedony tiepin of a zouave's head, and a carved head of a negress.

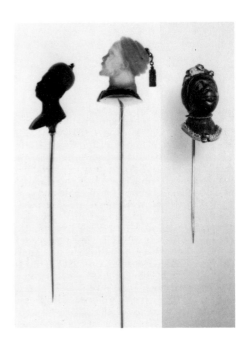

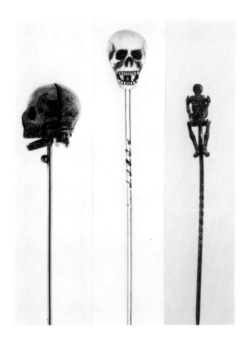

65. An enamelled death's head, with hinged jaw and rolling eyes, and another enamelled skull, and an enamelled skeleton.

66. (*below*) A carved gold head of a Gaul, French.

half-pearls, coral, faceted onyx or jet with a small compartment on either the front or back for a lock of hair; again, inscriptions were common. Between 1830 and 1860 onyx cameos were carved as forget-me-nots and the white relief on the black ground looked most effective against the cravat. An extremely popular motif of the 1840s was the serpent which coiled down the neckwear (fig. 50). A symbol of eternity, it was either of gold decorated with blue or black enamel or made entirely of plaited hair. Often the snake held a heart-shaped locket containing a lock of hair between its curling lips, or it was coiled around a stone such as onyx or carbuncle in a rather menacing mood, often with its very realistic scales enhanced by enamel. This motif, coiled around a nest of eggs, was used in

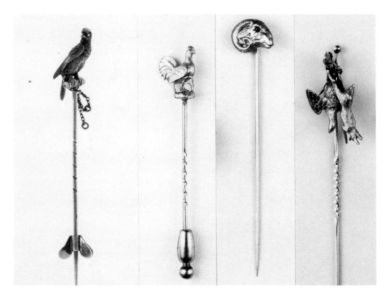

67. A collection of French carved gold tiepins in the form of birds and animals including a falcon, a cockerel, a ram's head, and a grouse and hare, possibly by H. Obry.

the French gold tiepins of the 1830s.

Jet was another popular material used for mourning jewels. A form of petrified wood found mainly in Whitby, this black symbol of death was carved into a variety of designs from crosses to cameos. It was used throughout the 19th century and although it was a very cheap material it soon became very effectively imitated by an even less costly material, black glass. This was moulded into many different shapes and motifs and often made very elegant tiepins.

During the second half of the 19th century the tiepin came in an oval form decorated with black enamel or carved onyx which could be further embellished with a single pearl or a rose diamond. Memorial tiepins held their place in the fashion scene throughout the 19th century and into the early part of the 20th, and there is an abundance of examples to suit all tastes.

A revival of classical jewellery was staged at the very beginning of the 19th century. It took the form mainly of carved intaglios and cameos. A cameo has the design carved in relief whereas the intaglio has the design carved into the stone. Napoleon was one of the main instigators in this revival. Antiquities fascinated him and he did not return from his campaigns in Italy empty handed. Ancient cameos and intaglios were among the many works of art he brought with him and these fine jewels were soon mounted and worn by the new French court to complement the classicism of their dress. In its simplicity and elegance the neo-classical style was far removed from the opulence and extravagance of the old royal court.

Although initially the majority of carved gems were genuine ancient pieces mounted in contemporary settings, the art of the carver was soon revived and 19th century craftsmen produced many examples, usually portraying classical scenes. These jewels were originally

68. A gold tiepin in the form of a parrot, pavé-set with turquoise.

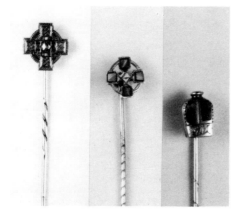

69. A collection of gold, silver, Scottish pebble and rose diamond tiepins including a whisky flask and two crosses.

43

70. A collection of gold and enamel tiepins by W. Essex and W. B. Ford.

carved from hardstones such as cornelian and agate (figs. 51 and 52) but as the century progressed materials which were cheaper and easier to carve were used. By the mid-19th century coral and shell cameos were in vogue (fig. 53). Italy was once again the prime source of these jewels, having both the natural materials and the skilled craftsmen to carry out the work, with Naples being the centre of the industry. For the shell cameo two varieties of shell producing white reliefs were used, one on a pink and the other on a brown ground. Designs were still in the classical mould and depicted gods and goddesses and other mythological characters as well as popular historical figures. Indeed cameos had become so popular that Italian workers living in England and France were also employed to produce them.

The 1860s and 1870s were the most popular for coral cameos (fig. 54). This very attractive material was also carved into small figures or animals (fig. 55) as well as appearing as small uncut polished branches (fig. 56). Another material used for cameos was lava from Pompeii, usually in muted shades of browns and greys or creams. The vogue for all these tiepins continued through the century. They were usually oval or rectangular and mounted in very plain precious or base metal settings.

Tourism was undoubtedly a major reason for the popularity of these carved jewels. The rapid advances made in transport and the Victorians' great urge to travel to the countries they read about in contemporary literature led to many people from all walks of life travelling abroad. As is still the case today, they wanted to return with souvenirs. Apart from cameo and intaglio tiepins the gentlemen had other choices. One of them was mosaic, another revival of an earlier craft. In this there are two distinct types, the Roman and the Florentine. The former is composed of a glass back inlaid with smaller pieces of coloured glass (fig. 57).

71. A gold, enamel and rose diamond tiepin designed as a pansy, a gold and enamel tiepin decorated with an enamel cherub; a gold and enamel tiepin of Bacchus, and a silver and jet tiepin, decorated with enamel.

72. A collection of gold and tinted crystal tiepins.

The tiepins, again usually oval or rectangular in shape, mainly depicted famous Italian landmarks or monuments. Florentine mosaic, or *pietra dura*, has a marble ground, more commonly black or dark blue, into which small pieces of cut stone such as coral, lapis lazuli and variously coloured marbles are inlaid (fig. 58). Popular motifs were birds, insects and flowers. Roman mosaics had re-emerged during the 18th century and by the 1840s they were very stylish for tiepins. Florentine mosaic became popular during the middle of the 19th century. The craze for these tiepins lasted until the turn of the century.

In the latter part of the century visitors to Switzerland and France could acquire finely carved ivory tiepins, often in the form of watchful stags and huntsmen or handsome horses; very delicate ivory flowers or cameos could also be purchased (fig. 59). Meanwhile, apart from the jeweller's concern with reviving past techniques and designs and catering for the tourist trade, other equally interesting and in some cases more original tiepins were being created.

In the 1820s semi-precious stones were in vogue and were often used in trefoil or flowerhead motifs, set with various quartz and mounted in plain gold settings or in *cannetille* (fig. 60). This is a very delicate form of gold work composed of scrolls of tightly coiled wire. It is named after the type of lace which it resembles. Between 1830 and 1840 the hand was a very popular motif, either carved from coral or in gilt metal or gold (fig. 61). The hand often displayed a rather reprimanding pointing finger adorned with a gem set ring, or the wrist was embellished with a bracelet. The hand was seen again later in the century carved in gold and clasping a gemstone (fig. 62), as was the popular eagle's claw (fig. 63).

Another part of the anatomy, the head, provided a popular design during the 1840s and 1850s on both sides of the Channel. It came in many guises varying from a blackamoor (fig. 64) to a bare skull (fig. 65). Some of the most attractive examples were skilfully carved in hardstones or gold and decorated with enamel. Indeed the head was part of the

73. (*above*) A gold and gem-set tiepin designed as a fly.

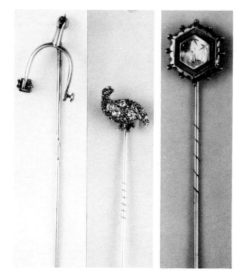

74. (*left*) A gold tiepin designed as a spur; and a rose diamond quail.

75. (*right*) A silver tiepin in Japanese taste.

47

French jeweller's repertoire of extremely striking tiepins throughout the second half of the 19th century (fig. 66). During this period he also used his craftsmanship to carve very life-like animals from rough nuggets of gold, and some very fine tiepins appeared in this form (fig. 67). One of the greatest exponents of this jewellery was Hubert Obry. A passionate countryman, he transformed his detailed observations of forest animals into stunning jewels and his tiepins included wild boar, hounds, stags and foxes. France also experienced a Gothic revival during this time and tiepins appeared in the form of mythological creatures such as griffins and dragons superbly carved in gold and in many cases decorated with enamel.

From 1840 until 1860 turquoise was at the forefront of fashion and appeared pavé-set in a variety of designs such as birds, flowerheads or in a simple button shape (fig. 68). The mid-

76. A collection of silver tiepins.

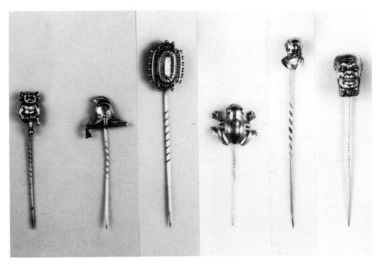

19th century finds of gold in the U.S.A. led to gold nuggets displayed as tiepins and these were produced well into the 1880s. At the same time, the war in Russia further enhanced the vogue for memorial jewels, while it popularized malachite, a bright green stone with dark markings found in the Ural mountains. Like the Russians, the European jewellers used it as an inlay in gold or silver and malachite tiepins usually came in a simple circular design or as a trefoil motif.

Queen Victoria again played an influential part in popularizing a type of jewellery from her beloved Scotland. Towards the middle of the century she had purchased Balmoral and she visited her heathered retreat whenever possible. Soon tiepins appeared in silver and gold inlaid with Scottish pebbles such as agates. Their designs included thistles, dirks, St. Andrew's crosses and even the odd whisky flask (fig. 69). The rich hazelnut hued quartz called cairngorm was often set in these pieces which were primarily the product of Edinburgh workshops. The mounts of the earlier examples were often embellished with chased floral motifs, while they became far plainer in the later 19th century.

Towards the middle of the century some very charming enamel tiepins came on to the market. Usually circular and mounted in gold they depicted mainly dogs and other domestic animals in very fine miniature. Two of the greatest exponents of this work were William Essex and William B. Ford (fig. 70). Both exhibited at the Royal Academy and William Essex was appointed miniature painter to the Queen in 1839. Their subjects were often copied from larger portraits on exhibition. They signed and dated their pieces on the reverse, which was counter-enamelled to prevent the metal buckling. Other artists followed this vogue, in some cases successfully, but more often the work was extremely poor. Throughout the 19th century enamel was an effective and popular means of decorating jewellery and an enormous variety of enam-

77. A gold, seed pearl, demantoid garnet and diamond tiepin designed as a flower.

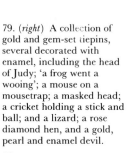

78. (*above*) A carved labradorite head of a monkey tiepin, and a carved labradorite head of Bacchus, the eyes set with rose diamonds.

elled tiepins appeared on the market (fig. 71). Sometimes the pieces were decorated entirely with enamel but often it was only used as a final embellishment.

Still on the theme of animals the 1860s saw a new and very effective jewel in the form of a tinted crystal intaglio which made an extremely attractive tiepin (fig. 72). A design is carved into the back of a cabochon crystal. This is then painted and backed by a thin sliver of mother of pearl. The subject appears as if frozen in a goldfish bowl. The designs of these tiepins mainly depicted animals and birds, mounted in gold within either plain or beaded borders. The back of the mount often bore the name of the subject, and in the case of racehorses, the dates of their victories. These too were not free from the imitator and later in the century rather crude prints were coloured, encased by cabochon glass and mounted in gilt metal, but it is usually easy to differentiate between the two.

These jewels were popular at the same time as the insect motif emerged. Diamond flies, bees, wasps and butterflies hovered with ever

79. (*right*) A collection of gold and gem-set tiepins, several decorated with enamel, including the head of Judy; 'a frog went a wooing'; a mouse on a mousetrap; a masked head; a cricket holding a stick and ball; and a lizard; a rose diamond hen, and a gold, pearl and enamel devil.

watchful cabochon ruby or sapphire eyes (fig. 73). By the 1870s Brazilian or South American beetles were mounted in gold, silver or gilt metal as tiepins. They are genuine creatures whose brightly coloured, rather metallic greenish-blue shells are as tough as many gemstones. The 1860s also saw the beginnings of the craze for sporting jewellery which became so popular around the turn of the century. Every animal or object connected with hunting, shooting or fishing appeared in the jeweller's window. Familiar tiepin designs were fox masks, horseshoes, hunting horns, fish and game birds (fig. 74). There was a vast range made from both expensive and cheap materials to cater for both ends of the market.

Silver jewels enjoyed a sudden and frenzied vogue from the late 1870s until the mid-1880s. This was partly due to such factors as the new discoveries of silver in the U.S.A. making it a more reasonably priced commodity, and to the rising price of gold. Tiepins were produced in a variety of shapes and designs which were either plain with a simple monogram or engraved with geometric or floral motifs. The

80. A gold and enamel doll with moveable limbs.

Japanese craze which flourished around this time gave rise to tiepins decorated with oriental flora and fauna, sometimes inlaid with pink gold or copper (fig. 75). The popularity of silver began to diminish in the early 1890s but by the mid-1890s the prolific Birmingham manufacturers had staged a strong comeback: a vast range of tiepins was created well into the 20th century. Silver was extremely popular for sporting motifs as well as for some of the more frivolous designs of the day (fig. 76).

Although the late 1880s and the 1890s saw many designs such as crescents, flowers and stars set with diamonds and other precious stones, it was also a period when the jeweller was eager to incorporate other more unusual gemstones into his pieces. Some of these possess interesting optical effects. The deman-

81. (*left*) A gold and gem-set tiepin designed as a knot.

82. (*right*) Two porcelain tiepins decorated with transfer prints of a lady and a cockerel.

52

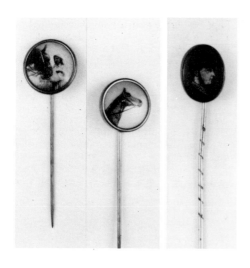

toid garnet, for example, was discovered in the Urals in the 1860s. It is a rich apple green colour and actually has more fire than a diamond, a property unfortunately hidden by its vibrant colour. Towards the end of the century tiepins appeared set with this highly attractive gem which could be used in conjunction with other stones, mounted alone or as, say, the eyes of a small reptile (fig. 77). The chrysoberyl catseye, of a brownish-green to honey-yellow colour, appears to have a thin strip of light moving across its surface as it is turned. This rather eye-catching effect is known as chatoyancy. During the 19th century it was still a relatively cheap gemstone and when mounted alone or within a border of diamonds it made a very exciting tiepin. Nowadays both of these gemstones are highly sought after and can be extremely expensive. The rather dreamy moonstone came to the jeweller's bench and was either carved, often to represent the man in the moon, or simply cut as a cabochon. Moonstones were set either in plain gold or star-shaped gem-set borders.

85. A transfer print of a lady on porcelain mounted as a tiepin, the reverse with a 'what the butler saw'.

A more unusual gemstone is the labradorite which, although basically of a greyish colour, shows enchanting flashes of blue and green and sometimes orange light when turned (fig. 78). This stone was either cut as a cabochon or carved as the head of a wild animal, sometimes further embellished with rose diamond eyes.

The single pearl or diamond formed an extremely popular tiepin during this period but more fun loving men were seen wearing a whole host of crazy designs (fig. 79). Gold dolls with moveable limbs, eagles' claws, skeletons, and bicycles, or the many sporting motifs all adorned the tie (fig. 80). Another very popular design of the day was the knot in its different forms (fig. 81).

The latter part of the century is notable for

86. A collection of gold, enamel and gem-set presentation tiepins.

tiepins from the art nouveau and Arts and Crafts jewellers. In England the Arts and Crafts movement encouraged the feeling of individualism in a jewel and sought to do away with mass production. The tiepins were usually silver and incorporated scroll or floral motifs decorated with enamels and on occasion gem set with stones such as peridots and amethysts. Liberty and Company produced some typical examples. The art nouveau tiepins were highly decorative and based on rather languid and sensuous lines. Motifs from nature seemed to be reborn and flowing with fresh blood. The tiepins were usually gold and were decorated with enamel, often taking the form of blossoming flowers or a rather curvaceous female. In America Tiffany was also designing tiepins in this style

87. A gold, ruby and diamond presentation tiepin by Fabergé, given to the station master at Wolferton (Sandringham) by Tsar Nicholas II.

88. Two diamond-set monogram tiepins.

89. A gem-set flag; a pink
pearl and diamond tiepin,
and a lapis lazuli and
diamond tiepin.

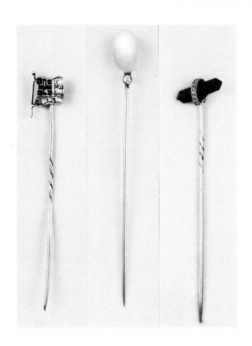

and in Russia even Fabergé was willing to put
his skilful hands to the task of designing such
jewels for men. These again were usually
enamelled and gem set.

The second half of the 19th century saw the
introduction of a large number of cheaper
versions of the tiepin, several of which have
already been mentioned. Porcelain tiepins
decorated with transfer prints (fig. 82) or
photograph prints (fig. 83) were produced in
vast quantities in a variety of designs as were
prints on paper which were mounted behind
glass (fig. 84). They were usually rather
crudely set in gilt metal or silver but many are
still interesting examples in their own right.
Porcelain tiepins were made all over the
Continent and often portrayed coy young
females in national costume. In fact some need

not have looked so innocent: on the reverse of some miniatures there is a peephole with a minute photograph which, if held up to the light, reveals a female in a far from prim pose (fig. 85). Versions of many of the other popular themes were also made in gilt metal and pastes.

Throughout the 19th century and well into the 20th presentation tiepins were made (fig. 86). Mainly they were the tinted crystal intaglios or gold, either plain, enamelled or gem set. Customarily they were made for members of the royal family or other dignitaries to present as gifts or as rewards for services rendered. They usually incorporated a monogram as well as the family crest and motto. Some are extremely attractive and the history of their origins often adds to the interest and desirability of these pieces. Other tiepins on these lines consisted of gem-set initials and these could be specially made to suit individual requirements (fig. 88).

Tiepin designs of the late 19th century generally continued into the early years of the 20th. By the end of the First World War they were showing less originality even though many were most stylish.

Simple geometric designs set with small gemstones neatly adorned the tie (fig. 89); flags unfurled and spades set with interestingly cut diamonds dug against it. But soon the age of fun, flair and novelty for the tiepin seemed to draw to a close. As men's clothes became more conventional and dowdy, so too did the tiepin, until it seemed almost to merge into obscurity. Fortunately today there seems to be a slight revival in the tiepin habit and one can but hope that more men take to wearing this interesting and eye-catching jewel.

THE fascinating quest for hatpins or tiepins to form a collection can provide
endless hours of enjoyment (figs. 90
and 91). It is only by seeing and examining as
many examples as possible that knowledge of
the subject can be increased and cemented.
The obvious places to look are in antique
markets and centres, antiques fairs, specialist
shops and auction rooms.

Naturally one learns from inevitable mis-
takes but the purchase of a 10× magnifying
lens, which is essential when looking at any

90. A silver hatpin designed
as a double-headed Pierrot;
and a gilt metal hatpin
designed as a strawberry.

91. A collection of early 20th century tiepins.

form of jewellery, can often help to reduce these sometimes costly errors. With its aid an object can be examined in detail and its flaws, if any, discovered.

In the case of both hatpins and tiepins always examine the part where the pin joins the head: the head may have been adapted from another type of jewel such as a brooch or a button, and traces of the original fittings may be visible. Lead solder can also be an indication of an alteration to the piece. In the case of gold pins it is usually very easy to detect any repairs as the colour of gold rarely matches perfectly. Assay and makers' marks on gold and silver are extremely helpful and these can be found either on the head or on the pin.

When purchasing a gem-set example, unless you have a knowledge of gemmology or the pin is so reasonably priced that you are willing to take a gamble that the stones are genuine, always buy from a reputable source where they do know their gems. Unfortunately many pastes and synthetic stones can appear extremely convincing to the untutored eye. A knowledge of the styles of cutting gems should also be obtained as the way in which a stone has been cut is often indicative of its age: a circular brilliant-cut diamond should not

92. A collection of hatpins on a hatpin stand.

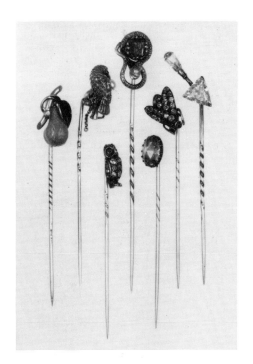

appear in an early 19th century tiepin. An ill-fitting setting around a stone is often a sign of a replacement. Your lens can prove invaluable in looking for these and other pointers.

Having formed your collection do treat it with the loving care it deserves. The perfection which attracted you to a piece in the first place can be obliterated in a few moments of care-lessness. All gemstones possess a degree of hardness, diamonds being the hardest, and harder stones can easily scratch softer stones, so never keep them in a place where they can rub against each other. The fragility of certain materials such as enamel or carved coral and ivory should speak for itself.

Hatpins and tiepins can be found in an

enormous variety of designs and materials at prices to suit practically every size of pocket and almost every taste. In the case of both forms of jewellery it is virtually impossible to give any indication of price as this not only depends on the material used but also on how skilfully it has been employed and how aesthetically pleasing or popular is the design. Naturally examples made by famous jewellers or from precious stones or metals may prove both expensive and difficult to find, but at the other end of the scale it is still possible to assemble an interesting collection of pieces for less than £50.

The pleasure derived from building up your collection can perhaps only be equalled by the joy of seeing it well displayed. Attractive holders can be purchased for your hatpins, and your tiepin, when not in a case, can be shown off in the most appropriate place possible – on your tie. Both hatpins and tie-pins are forms of jewellery which played important roles in the male and female dress of earlier days, and they were basically created to be worn and enjoyed.

Books for Further Reading

Becker, Vivienne. *Antique and 20th Century Jewellery*.
Flower, Margaret. *Victorian Jewellery*, New York, 1951.
Gere, Charlotte. *Victorian Jewellery Design*, London, 1972.
Hinks, Peter. *Nineteenth Century Jewellery*, Faber & Faber, London, 1975.
Holme, Charles (Editor). *Modern Designs in Jewellery and Fans*, Offices of *The Studio*, London, Paris and New York, 1902.
Turner Wilcox, R. *The Mode in Hats and Headdress*, 1959.
Vever, Henri. *La Bijouterie Française au XIXe Siècle*, Paris, 1908.

Acknowledgements

The author and publishers would like to thank the following for permission to use the photographs in this book:
Olivia Bostock 49, 51; Christie, Manson & Woods Ltd. 23, 24; Moira Cohen 64, 65; John Henniker-Wilson 66; James Hodges 50, 55, 67, 76, 78, 79, 89; M. Keays 41, 43, 67, 71, 76, 80, 81, 82, 88; Lis, London 12–15, 18–21, 25, 29, 31–33, 37, 40, 90; Massada Antiques Ltd. 2–4, 52, 53, 55, 57, 58, 67, 69, 77, 79; Mrs H. K. Matthews 5, 6, 45; Phillips Auctioneers 7–11, 16, 17, 22, 27, 28, 30, 34, 36, 38, 39, 42, 92; Messrs Sotheby's 1, 35, 44, 48, 57, 58, 60, 62–65, 67, 69–74, 78, 79, 86, 89, 91, 93; Tessiers, London 74; Wartski Jewellers Ltd. 26, 87.
   The author would particularly like to thank Joanna Smith for her help with the photography.

Index

Bold numbers refer to illustrations

0278683 RHODES A.M.
12.84
BW

Hat Pins And Tie
Pins.
2.95

First published 1982

−0. DEC. 1984

to Raymond

Cover illustration shows a selection of early 20th century
hatpins of materials including silver, brass,
enamel and paste; and a selection of
19th and early 20th century tiepins of precious
and semi-precious materials. Photo: Joanna Smith.

The Publishers apologize to the National Magazine Co. Ltd. for
unintentionally using their trade mark 'Antique Collector' in the
series title of this book which has no connection with their
'Antique Collector' magazine.

ISBN 0−7188−2540−3

Printed in Great Britain by
Mackays of Chatham Ltd